Successful Strategies for Pursuing National Board Certification

Other Books by this Author in the WHAT WORKS! Series

Successful Writing Strategies for National Board Certification (2014)

Successful Strategies for Middle Childhood Generalists Pursuing National Board Certification (2012)

Successful Strategies in Pursuing National Board Certification (2011)

Successful Strategies for Pursuing National Board Certification

Version 3.0, Components 1 and 2

Bobbie Faulkner

ROWMAN & LITTLEFIELD
Lanham • Boulder • New York • London

Published by Rowman & Littlefield
A wholly owned subsidiary of The Rowman & Littlefield Publishing Group, Inc.
4501 Forbes Boulevard, Suite 200, Lanham, Maryland 20706
www.rowman.com

Unit A, Whitacre Mews, 26-34 Stannary Street, London SE11 4AB

British Library Cataloguing in Publication Information Available

Library of Congress Cataloging-in-Publication Data

Names: Faulkner, Bobbie, 1947-
Title: Successful strategies for National Board Certification, version 3.0, components 1 and 2 / Bobbie Faulkner.
Description: Lanham : Rowman & Littlefield, 2015.
Identifiers: LCCN 2015037990| ISBN 9781475824827 (pbk. : alk. paper) | ISBN 9781475824834 (electronic)
Subjects: LCSH: Teachers--Certification--Standards--United States--Study guides. | Teaching--Standards--United States--Study guides.
Classification: LCC LB1771 .F365 2015 | DDC 371.12076--dc23 LC record available at http://lccn.loc.gov/201503799

∞ ™ The paper used in this publication meets the minimum requirements of American National Standard for Information Sciences Permanence of Paper for Printed Library Materials, ANSI/NISO Z39.48-1992.

Printed in the United States of America

Contents

Preface ix

Acknowledgments xi

Introduction 1

1 What Is National Board Certification? 3

2 Building Your Foundation 7

3 Getting Started and Getting Support 13

4 Component 1: Content Knowledge: A Computer-Based Assessment of Content and Pedagogical Practices 21

5 Component 2: Differentiation in Instruction: Showing Accomplished Teaching through Student Work 29

6 Writing for the National Board 39

Appendix 47

About the Author 51

Preface

In 2014, the National Board for Professional Teaching Standards (NBPTS) began rolling out their latest revision of the National Board Certification process, sometimes informally referred to as Version 3.0. During the 2014–2015 cycle, Component 1 and Component 2 were released. Component 3 will be released during the 2015–2016 cycle, and Component 4 will be unveiled during the 2016–2017 cycle.

This publication is written to support candidates doing the new, updated, 3.0 version of Components 1 and 2 and will not be accurate if you began the certification process before 2014.

Acknowledgments

I would like to offer special thanks to those who have contributed significantly to my National Board Certification journey. From Scottsdale, I owe appreciation to Nancy Creighton Brown, former Career Ladder Specialist, whose open mind, vision, and dedication to Scottsdale teachers allowed National Board Certification to take root and grow in Scottsdale. Former Superintendent Dr. John Baracy and the Governing Board demonstrated financial support for National Board Certified Teachers. Dr. Andi Fourlis, Dr. Jeff Thomas, Wendy Allen, and now Dr. Karen Benson have also been instrumental to National Board support in Scottsdale. A special thank you goes to L. Kelly Mueller, whose fantastic website, The Power of Accomplished Teaching (ecgen.org), and critiques were invaluable.

Finally, I want to acknowledge Dr. Kathy Wiebke, Director of the Arizona K–12 Center for her inspiration and dedication to the National Board Certification process in Arizona. All of her staff work hard to make a difference for Arizona educators. Thanks to their dedication, in 2015, Arizona has over 1,100 National Board Certified Teachers and the number continues to grow.

Introduction

The *What Works!* book series for National Board Certification candidates began with an off-the-cuff remark. "You ought to write a book," a fellow Candidate Support Provider (CSP) said one day after a workshop for candidates. So that's what I did. This publication is actually the fourth in the What Works! series, but the first to address the 3.0 version.

WHAT WORKS! Successful Strategies for Pursuing National Board Certification Version 3.0 Components 1 and 2 replaces information in the original series. This is a supplement to the entire body of information and instructions provided to candidates from the National Board for Professional Teaching Standards (NBPTS). Information and directions in the official documents are always the final word and trump any other source.

WHAT WORKS! Successful Strategies for Pursuing National Board Certification Version 3.0 Components 1 and 2 is *not* endorsed by the NBPTS or any other entity involved in the National Board Certification process. It is not meant to be a "Cliff Notes"–type publication one can use to circumvent the NBPTS documents and instructions.

WHAT WORKS! Successful Strategies for Pursuing National Board Certification Version 3.0 Components 1 and 2 contains tips, opinions, information, documents, and examples that have been created solely for the purposes of demonstration and are neither approved nor endorsed by the NBPTS. Keep in mind that:

- The author is not a trained assessor and does not imply that any sample writing would score well and/or lead to certification according to the NBPTS rubrics.
- All samples are hypothetical, fabricated, made up, and are not from actual Components. They cannot be copied for use within a Component.

- *WHAT WORKS! Successful Strategies for Pursuing National Board Certification Version 3.0 Components 1 and 2* is as current as I can make it. However, it is the responsibility of the candidate to be informed of the current NBPTS requirements in case directions change.

This update, *WHAT WORKS! Successful Strategies for Pursuing National Board Certification Version 3.0 Components 1 and 2*, is a labor of love for my fellow educators and National Board candidates. It is my hope that the information will make your journey to National Board Certification just a little easier, more meaningful, and lead to certification.

Chapter One

What Is National Board Certification?

Six-Word Memoir: Know your Standards. Know them well! —Britney, NC

NBPTS BACKGROUND AND HISTORY

National Board Certification is a national *voluntary* system that certifies teachers who meet a set of high and rigorous standards for what accomplished teachers should know and be able to do. This certification system was developed by the National Board for Professional Teaching Standards (NBPTS) and put in place in 1987 following recommendations from the Carnegie reports *A Nation at Risk* and *A Nation Prepared.*

The National Board has developed high, rigorous, research-based standards to measure the effectiveness of a teacher's practice. The process involves an extensive series of performance-based assessments that include student work samples, written commentaries, videotapes, thorough analysis of the teacher's classroom practice, and the impact on student learning. In addition, teachers complete a series of multiple choice and essay-type exercises that probe their depth of knowledge of their subject matter.

The work is based on long-established research that identifies and recognizes sound educational practices that result in student learning. The NBPTS has commissioned more than 140 studies and papers on the value of the certification process as well as its standards and assessment. The process has also been validated by a number of independent studies.

THE FIVE CORE PROPOSITIONS

The Core Propositions are the heart of the National Board process. They outline the expectations and values for what *accomplished* teachers should know and be able to do, and are the umbrella under which the other elements of the National Board Certification process are organized. Accomplished teaching implies going *above and beyond* what is typically expected of the average teacher. The Propositions describe skills in the following areas:

- *Proposition 1: Commitment to Students.* Accomplished teachers know the developmental levels of their students, believe that all students can learn regardless of background, and use their knowledge to design effective instruction for all students and a variety of learning styles.
- *Proposition 2: Knowledge of Subject.* Building upon their knowledge of students, accomplished teachers advance their own understanding of their content area and develop a wide range of strategies to set high and worthwhile goals to teach that subject matter to their students.
- *Proposition 3: Manage and Monitor Student Learning.* Accomplished teachers understand how to manage, motivate, monitor, and assess student learning by planning appropriate learning sequences to achieve the desired outcomes and adjusting instruction as needed. Accomplished teachers also know how to structure the learning environment for optimum learning.
- *Proposition 4: Think Systematically about Their Teaching and Learn from Experience.* Accomplished teachers analyze student learning and reflect on their teaching practice. They then determine the next set of high and worthwhile goals, implement appropriate instruction, and continue the analysis and reflection cycle.
- *Proposition 5: Teachers Are Members of Learning Communities.* Accomplished teachers collaborate with other professionals, parents, and their larger community to support and enhance student learning.

The Standards: There are twenty-five certificates that cover many subject areas and student development levels. Each contains a set of Standards, which, along with the Five Core Propositions, form the foundation of National Board Certification. The Standards identify specific knowledge, skills, and attitudes that support accomplished practice, while emphasizing the holistic nature of teaching. They identify how a teacher's professional judgment is reflected in action and how they reflect the Five Core Propositions.

To achieve National Board Certification and be considered an accomplished teacher, a candidate must show *clear, convincing, and consistent evidence that his or her teaching practice reflects the Standards*. Understanding the Standards and how to demonstrate them in practice provides evidence of accomplished teaching.

WHAT WORKS: UNDERSTANDING THE STANDARDS

- *Read* the Standards multiple times. Pay attention to the examples included in each.
- *Think* about how you already incorporate the Standards.
- *Highlight* things you already do regularly in one color, things you do sometimes in a second color, and things you rarely or never do in a third color. This will help you recognize your strengths and what might be bolstered in your practice.
- *Show* clear, consistent, convincing evidence that your teaching is based on the Standards.

WHY IT WORKS: The Standards were developed to identify accomplished teaching. Candidates are expected to show evidence of the Standards within their teaching.

THE PROCESS

National Board Certification is a rigorous process that may take up to three years to achieve once all Components in the 3.0 version are introduced. Candidates are asked to:

- *Demonstrate* within their teaching practice the rigorous Standards discussed.
- *Show* leadership, collaboration, learning, reflective practice, and professionalism.
- *Prepare* written Components that document their teaching practice.
- *Focus* on analysis of student work samples, classroom practice, professional development, collaboration, and leadership.
- *Make* videotapes of the teacher working with his/her class (Component 3).
- *Complete* a series of subject specific multiple choice and essay tests at a Testing Center to document knowledge of their subject area.

National Board Certification is the highest, most comprehensive voluntary professional development experience available to teachers. Examining their teaching practice and professional accomplishments in depth provides teachers a professional growth experience unlike any other.

Chapter Two

Building Your Foundation

Six-Word Memoir: The AAT: Backbone of Accomplished Lessons.
—Russell, VT

WHO IS AN ACCOMPLISHED TEACHER?

In a nutshell, an accomplished teacher is one who goes *above and beyond* what is typically expected. Accomplished teachers practice exceptional, skilled teaching. They have a strong knowledge base of subject matter and pedagogy, demonstrate complex, nuanced professional work, and consistently meet rigorous standards of practice. Accomplished teachers are committed to their students, know their subjects and how to teach them, know how to manage and monitor student learning, reflect on their practice and learn from their experience, and are learners, collaborators, and leaders within their professional communities.

Accomplished teachers are teachers just like you, who try their best every day to meet their students' needs, keep current with pedagogy and subject knowledge, and work with others in their schools and districts to create an environment conducive to supporting the healthy growth and development of their students academically, socially, and emotionally.

WHAT IS ACCOMPLISHED TEACHING?

Accomplished teaching is the entwined double helix of knowing your subject and how to teach it. The two strands are closely interwoven and almost seamlessly connected. Accomplished teaching combines both the art and craft of teaching along with a solid knowledge base of content and child development.

Accomplished teaching means planning and demonstrating effective instruction for *these students, at this time, in this place*. The National Board describes accomplished teaching practices in the National Board Standards developed for each certificate. They are the specific teaching behaviors accomplished teachers demonstrate within their teaching practice. As a candidate for National Board Certification, you need to show evidence of the Standards in your teaching practice.

THE ARCHITECTURE OF ACCOMPLISHED TEACHING

The Architecture of Accomplished Teaching (AAT) is the NB version of an accomplished lesson/unit plan. It is a double helix representation of accomplished teaching practice as it applies to the lessons candidates use in Components 2 and 3, and in the Component 1 exercises. It is designed to give a visual of how the accomplished teaching of units of study and lessons are organized. It is an underused tool that can add greatly to the understanding of the National Board process and what the National Board is looking for. Many prompts you'll respond to in your Written Commentary are connected to specific steps in AAT.

Candidates often lament that if they just knew what the National Board "wanted," they'd know what to do for each Component. In truth, candidates who understand AAT and use its structure as the basis for planning their lesson sequences will demonstrate what the assessors want—evidence of accomplished teaching. This tool is found in your GENERAL Instructions. I suggest posting a copy of it near your computer for frequent and easy reference.

WHAT WORKS! STUDYING THE ARCHITECTURE OF ACCOMPLISHED TEACHING

Step 1: Start with knowledge of your students. *(Proposition 1)*

- Who are they? Where are they now in their learning? Where should you begin?
- What knowledge about your students influenced the goals you set?
- How do you incorporate this knowledge into your lesson planning?
- What will success for your students look like?

Step 2: Continue setting high, worthwhile goals. *(Proposition 1)*

- How do the goals you set connect to your Standards and Component instructions?

- How do the goals fit in the sequence of your overarching goals?
- What do you want your students to know at the end of the lesson or unit?

Step 3: Implement Instruction. *(Proposition 2)*

- What approaches do you plan to use to accomplish your goals?
- In what sequence might you plan the strategies you plan to use?
- How will the strategies you choose support your students learning?
- What is your rationale for implementing instruction this way?
- What criteria might you use to decide if and when to use another strategy?

Step 4: Evaluate Student Learning. *(Proposition 3)*

- How will you assess student learning?
- Why did you choose these methods for these students at this time, in this setting?
- What evidence will let you know if the instruction was successful—or not?
- What, if anything, did the assessment(s) tell you about your instruction?
- Where will you go next?

Step 5: Reflect on the effectiveness of your lesson design and decisions. *(Proposition 4)*

- How do you know whether you made the right choices?
- What was successful and what was not?
- How could students reflect on their own learning?

Step 6: Set new, high, worthwhile goals. *(Proposition 4)*

- How will you decide when it is time to move on in the lesson sequence?
- What indicators will you use to set new goals?

SSTARS: Here is an acronym to jog your memory.

- **S**tudents: Know your students and how they learn. Proposition 1
- **S**et high, worthwhile, and appropriate goals. Propositions 1 and 2
- **T**each using appropriate, effective strategies. Propositions 2 and 3

- **A**ssess student progress using a variety of evaluation types and forms. Proposition 3
- **R**eflect on your teaching and your students' progress. Proposition 4
- **S**tart the process again.
- **S**ee Appendix for a SSTARS lesson plan template.

WHY IT WORKS!: The elements of AAT provide a complete lesson/unit plan that will have the greatest impact on student learning.

WHAT WORKS! Knowing When to Use the Writing Styles

- Use mainly *descriptive* writing with some analysis for Steps 1, 2, and 3.
- Use mainly *analytical* writing for Step 4.
- Use mainly *analytical and reflective* writing for Steps 5 and 6.

WHY IT WORKS!: Use the Architecture of Accomplished Teaching to discern the nuances in the prompts. This will help you use the appropriate writing style for each. The prompts align with the Architecture's steps and using it will help you find evidence of your thinking and teaching to write about.

The Scoring Rubrics

The Scoring Rubrics are underutilized resources that can be a life saver. The assessors have these documents beside them as they score your work. How your Component will be scored is not a secret! Everything you need to show evidence of is listed in a user-friendly bullet format.

WHAT WORKS! Including the 3-Cs of Evidence

- *Clear:* Anyone who reads your Written Commentary should be able to understand what you are saying. You've explained acronyms and educational terms. The sequence of events can be easily followed. Your writing is readable and makes sense.
- *Consistent:* Your writing needs an element of continuity. Don't say one thing in the first paragraph, and then contradict it later. Numbers must add up, timelines need to be accurate and illustrate "flow," and your data shared honestly.
- *Convincing:* Present the case that you are an accomplished teacher. This means you present your evidence, and it is believable and achievable. The best way to do this is to include specific examples, documentation, and verification. Including specific examples provides stronger, more convincing evidence. Evidence = Examples.

WHAT WORKS! Studying the Rubrics

- Read all of the levels from Level 4 down to Level 1. You will see a great difference in the quality of evidence present in each one.
- Concentrate on the Level 4 Rubric. Keep it beside you as you write so you'll know exactly what evidence you need to show. Be sure you have evidence for each bullet. Notice how it aligns with parts of AAT. Also pay attention to presenting specific examples.
- Use the Level 4 Rubric to self-assess each Component. Go through it bullet by bullet to be sure you've included everything you need. If something is missing, put it in!

WHY IT WORKS!: Using effective tools such as AAT, the Scoring Rubrics will make the process less frustrating and more meaningful because you'll know where to go for guidance and clarification. Make these tools work for you!

Chapter Three

Getting Started and Getting Support

Six-Word Memoir: Start Sooner—NOW—rather than later! —Lynn, AZ

THE STANDARDS, THE LINGO, AND THE COMPONENT REQUIREMENTS

New candidates often don't know where to start. They know they're embarking on a unique journey, but aren't sure what steps to take first. If this describes you, read on.

- Refresh your understanding of the Five Core Propositions. They are the umbrella under which all other National Board documents are organized.
- Read and internalize the Standards for your certificate. You must know what they look like in practice, and how you use them in your practice.
- Read your *General Instructions*. This is an underused resource with a wealth of information that is easy to refer to later.
- Study the *Learning Portfolio-Related Terms* (GLOSSARY) section in the General Instructions to become familiar with National Board "language" that is specialized and specific to the National Board process. Certain phrases are used repeatedly in your instructions and the glossary is where many are defined.
- Familiarize yourself with the *Overview* at the beginning of each Component of your instructions to understand the content of each Component.
- Study the *What Do I Need to Do?* section of each Component for a list of requirements.

WHAT WORKS!: Familiarize yourself with the Component Instructions, National Board "language," and structure of the Components to give yourself the "big picture" and the tools and confidence to move forward.

NAVIGATING THE NATIONAL BOARD WEBSITE

The National Board website located at **www.boardcertifiedteachers.org** contains a wealth of information. Everything you want and need to know to prepare for and complete Components 1 and 2 is there. But it is a complex site. Here is a guide to its major components and the documents you'll need to find, download, print, and reference. On the homepage, click on the *For Candidates* tab.

For Candidates

If you became a candidate for the first time in 2014 or later, in the Menu Sidebar on the left side, click on *First-time and Returning Candidates*. This takes you to a page with a *Matrix* and other important documents including:

- Component 1: At-A-Glance
- Component 2: At-A-Glance
- Guide to National Board Certification
- Choosing the Right Certificate Area
- Forms including *Request for Testing Accommodations; Eligibility Verification Forms; Adult and Student Release Forms; and the Assessment Center Policy Guidelines*. It will be important to look thoroughly at all of these.

The Matrix

The Matrix contains the Certificates, Standards, and Instructions for all first-time candidates. You'll find:

- Certificate Areas: Disciplines and Developmental Levels
- Component Instructions include Scoring Rubrics and other Forms you'll submit.
- Certificate Areas Standards
- Documents may be added and/or revised periodically, so always use the most current resource.

These documents become your resources for mapping your way through the process.

WHAT WORKS! Be familiar with the documents and resources you need to complete Components 1 and 2. This will save you time and grief!

WHY THIS WORKS! Knowing where to go quickly for information is one way to work smart!

ORGANIZING YOUR NATIONAL BOARD MATERIALS

Once you have a basic overview of the Components, it's time to implement some organizational strategies to help keep the myriad of written commentary drafts, paper piles, and artifacts you'll assemble in some kind of order. Here are several systems candidates have used successfully. Pick one or a combination that suits your own style and work habits.

WHAT WORKS! Organizing KISS Options: *K*eep *I*t *S*uper *S*imple!

- Spiral-bind each set of Component instructions. You'll end up with two "books" that are an easy to carry reference. They are also sturdy and will stand up to heavy use. Your school may have a spiral-binding machine, or go to an office supply store.
- Keep instructions in a binder sectioned for each Component. On the plus side, this keeps all instructions in one place. Binders can be heavy and awkward to carry but it's a familiar organizational system for many candidates.
- Use a file box with sections or hanging folders for each Component and for student work.

WHY IT WORKS! Following a *KISS* system will be a lifesaver. You won't waste hunting for lost work. Designate a place for your work—and keep it there!

WHAT WORKS! Organizing Your Written Commentary on Your Computer

- Get comfortable with your computer—it will become your best friend.
- Use a reliable word processing program.
- Follow all instructions as to font, type size, line spacing, margins, headers, and footers.
- Label each draft with the date. This will assure you are working on the latest version.
- Create a folder for each Component and save drafts in their appropriate place.

- Periodically print out drafts or back them up on a flash drive/memory stick you can use on any computer. This step will save you a lot of stress if your computer crashes or your laptop is lost or stolen.
- Remember: *save early, save often, and save everything!* Back up your files frequently.

WHY IT WORKS! Doing everything you can to keep your writing accessible and safe is prudent and smart. Nothing is worse than losing what you've worked so hard to produce!

WHAT WORKS! Organizing Your Time

Figuring out how to organize your time is by far the most difficult challenge. As you well know, teachers are incredibly busy both at work and at home. Family and work continually compete for your time and energy. The more Components you work on, the more important time management is. Here are some strategies successful candidates have used to help them cope with the time demands that National Board Certification places on them:

- Say no—to at least *some* things! Cut back on committees and school responsibilities where possible.
- Learn to say no at home too. Delegate chores and activities. This is not the year to become Team Parent for all of your kids' sports teams and activities. Spread the joy and let some other mom or dad take a turn.
- Set aside a designated daily or weekly work and writing period. Some candidates arrange for their spouse to be in charge of the family on Saturday or Sunday afternoon, or for one weeknight. Other candidates stay late at school once a week or go to their classroom to work on the weekend. This is especially important from January to your deadline date.
- Consider arranging a weekend away from home so you can work undisturbed. Go to a hotel, a cabin or house-sit for a friend who is away—anywhere you can be alone; *or* send your family away!
- In the weeks before the deadline, you'll need additional time to finish and polish your Component writing.
- Create a flexible and realistic timeline and do your best to stick to it.

More Strategies

- Avoid procrastination; it will come back to haunt you. Some candidates say they work better under pressure, and that may be true *for a few*. But in the National Board process you can't quickly dash off a paper and produce a quality product. Component 2 requires a great quantity of quality evidence collected over time, and putting together a successful product is too complex to be done in a hurry.

- Wait to work on Component 1 until after you've submitted your other Component(s) work to be scored.
- At the time of this writing, only Components 1 and 2 are available. If you become a candidate in 2015 or after, you may be working on Components 3 and/or 4 as well, so you will need to juggle time to work on multiple Components simultaneously.
- Look at your academic scope and sequence and begin to map out units for your Component 2.
- Look at Component 2 and earmark lessons you teach that will fulfill the requirements.
- Start researching if you need to show something you aren't familiar with—for example, inquiry science or writing strategies.
- Start early and save everything. Save work from multiple students.

WHY IT WORKS! Organizing your time wisely can be a make or break factor in the quality of your submission.

Build a Support System: Cohort Support

When National Board Certification began, candidates were few and far between, both in numbers and location. It wasn't unusual for someone to be the only candidate in their entire state. Fortunately, few candidates face that kind of isolation today. Thanks to National Board Certified Teachers who have certified in the past, a continuum of support has developed across the country. Candidate support systems may be available in or near your school district.

If you are in a cohort you will work with a Candidate Support Provider (CSP) or facilitator who will guide your group and be obligated to provide and uphold ethical candidate support according to NBPTS guidelines.

CSPs Responsibilities:

- Help candidates understand the instructions and process more clearly.
- Help candidates think more clearly and deeply about their teaching practice.
- Help candidates learn to analyze the evidence presented.
- Help candidates engage in self-evaluation.
- Offer patience and encouragement.
- Guide candidates toward making their own decisions about evidence.
- Meet regularly with the candidate cohort and encourage peer collaboration.

- Share knowledge, skills, and experiences.
- Listen non-judgmentally.
- Ask probing questions.
- Maintain confidentiality.

CSPs Cannot:

- Guarantee a certifying score.
- Tell candidates their writing is wrong, flawed, not good enough, or that a Component will or will not score well.
- Make a judgment call about Component instructions that seem unclear.
- Share NBCT writing or videos as teaching examples or tools.
- "Make" candidates into accomplished teachers or a National Board Certified Teacher.
- Create evidence for candidates or tell them how to write the Written Commentary.
- Tell candidates which students to feature, which student work to submit (Component 2), which videos to submit, or which segment of a video "will work" (Component3) for sure.
- Tell how to revise, edit, or fix writing.

If you participate in a cohort, you have responsibilities too, both to yourself and to the group.

Candidates Responsibilities:

- Make an investment in time and attend scheduled meetings.
- Share fears, concerns, and issues.
- Continually read, review, and apply the standards.
- Bring work and questions to sessions.
- Keep to established timelines.
- Accept feedback in a professional manner.
- Study the Component instructions.
- Come to meetings prepared.
- Maintain confidentiality.
- Commit time to the process.
- Celebrate steps along the way.

WHAT WORKS! If you don't have a cohort, you can still find support. Try these ideas:

- Form your own cohort. If there are other candidates in your district or area organize a monthly meeting. Consider rotating the location so all candidates host the group.
- Meet with other candidates outside your regular cohort meeting dates.
- Find online support. There are a number of National Board support groups on the Web, and most are free:

  www.proteacher.net—all certificate areas
  www.teachers.net—all certificate areas
  MC-GEN@yahoogroups.com
  early-middleliteracy@yahoogroups.com
  exceptional-needs@yahoogroups.com
  emcart@yahoogroups.com
  www.ecgen.org—for ECGens, MCGens, and Literacy candidates: $40/year

Many of these sites have chats and resource files you can access.

WHY IT WORKS! Collaborating with others gives you a sounding board and a place to ask questions and hear others' perspectives. Getting organized with a system that is user-friendly may take some trial and error. Once you find one that works for you, you'll feel more secure about moving forward.

Chapter Four

Component 1: Content Knowledge

A Computer-Based Assessment of Content and Pedagogical Practices

Six-Word Memoir: So much to say . . . so little space. —Samantha, NY

OVERVIEW: THE PURPOSE OF THE COMPONENT 1 EXERCISES

Component 1: Content Knowledge is a computer-based assessment requiring candidates to demonstrate knowledge of content and pedagogical practices for their teaching content area/subject. Candidates must demonstrate knowledge of developmentally appropriate content, which is necessary for teaching across the full age range and ability levels of the chosen certificate area. While Components 2 and 3 are all about your teaching practice—what you *do*—Component 1 examines what you *know* about your content as outlined in the NBPTS Standards. Component 1 can be completed at any time during the process. Being an accomplished teacher implies mastery of your disciplinary content, so the exercises:

- Focus on knowledge of *content and curriculum* across facets of your discipline.
- Focus on themes, ideas, and principles that represent core concepts and curriculum within a discipline.
- Ask you to demonstrate content and pedagogical knowledge with responses to exercises developed and designed by practicing professionals in your certificate area.
- Cover the entire age range of the certificate.

- Allow you to show knowledge of developmentally appropriate content across the full spectrum of your certificate.

The Component 1 Document explains the types of exercises and contains samples. The nature of the exercises and prompts in the Component 1 exercises varies among certificates, but all are divided into two types of exercises:

- Selected Response Exercise (Multiple Choice Questions)
- Constructed Response Exercises

Selected Response Items

"Selected Response" is a fancy term for multiple choice. Each certificate's assessment will contain approximately forty-five of this type of item. The Component 1 Document found on the National Board website gives you five practice items and an answer key. Each item is followed by four choices. If you are unsure of the correct response, narrow your choices to the two most probable answers. You can leave items unanswered, then go back later to make your final choice.

The Component 1 Document contains a chart to show the Standards the questions are connected to and the percent of questions connected to each Standard. For example, in the Early Childhood Generalist (ECGen) certificate, of the forty-five questions, approximately 30 percent (13.5 questions) connect to the ECGen Standards I and III, 35 percent (15.75) connect to Standards IV and VI, and 35 percent (15.75) to Standard IV. Of course, there can't be a fraction of a question, so the exact numbers may be adjusted. See your Component 1 Document for samples in your certificate area. Here are some key features to keep in mind:

- The Selected Response items cover the entire age range of the certificate.
- You are expected to demonstrate knowledge of developmentally appropriate content and pedagogy across the full range of your certificate.
- The items may cover both content knowledge and pedagogy.

Constructed Response Items

This is the "essay question" part of the assessment. In this section you will construct responses to three exercises, each representing a scenario that could occur within a teaching context or, in the case of the Math certificate, to solve problems. All exercises in all certificate areas follow the same structure:

- Introduction: A brief description of the exercise
- Criteria for Scoring: The Level 4 Rubric used to evaluate your response.
- Directions: How to use the computer to view the exercise.
- Stimulus: The actual scenario and/or resource used as the basis for your response. Not all certificate areas and not all exercises contain a stimulus.

Certificate Specific Examples

EC/MC Generalist; EC/MC Literacy; Reading/Language Arts; EC/YA ENS

These certificates link content to pedagogy. Knowing *how* to teach the concept *is* the content. The exercises may ask the candidate to:

- Analyze student responses to a stimulus/topic.
- Analyze, identify, and interpret student misconceptions/errors about a topic.
- Describe thorough, detailed, and appropriate instructional strategies and materials to correct misconceptions and/or extend understanding of the topic.
- Plan worthwhile goals and a developmentally appropriate instructional sequence, based on AAT that will accomplish the goals.
- Integrate another subject into the instruction.
- Provide a thorough, detailed rationale to justify decisions that fits these students, at this time, in this setting.

Science; Mathematics; Social Studies–History

These certificates may have exercises that emphasize connections between specialty areas and another context within the discipline, as well as your breadth of knowledge across the disciplines. Pedagogy is less important than the depth and breadth of content knowledge.

- Science certificates allow candidates to choose their area of specialty in Component 1.
- Math certificates have exercises that address specific areas including algebra, calculus, discrete mathematics, geometry, statistics and data analysis and technology.
- The Social Studies–History certificates ask you to demonstrate the breadth of your knowledge using graphics and documents in the areas of US History, World History, Political Science, Economics, and Geography.

These are just a few examples to illustrate the nature of the exercises/prompts found in various certificate areas. The Component 1 Document contains detailed information about the prompts for your certificate. This information guide is crucial for your preparation.

HOW TO STUDY FOR COMPONENT 1

- Start by reading the Component 1 Document thoroughly. It contains a wealth of information to help you understand the exercises. The samples and practice exercises provide the starting point.
- Make a "nutshell" for each exercise. This will break the prompts into bite-sized chunks that will make it easier to grasp what you'll be asked to do in each exercise. Create a chart or matrix for each exercise. Make a column for each part of the exercises: Introduction, Criteria for Scoring, and add a column detailing the VERBS used in the explanation and Rubric. Analyze the following chart of exercises from three Certificate areas:

Table 4.1.

HEALTH: Exercise 2	Criteria	Stimulus	Verbs
Demonstrate the content knowledge and skills necessary to manage healthy and unhealthy relationships	Identify knowledge/ skills to address a student question; detailed explanation; identify two sources	Student question	demonstate identify explain
AYA/ELA: Exercise 1 Identify literary genres and analyze the connection between author's choices and literary devices. Discuss genre, purpose, theme, and meaning	Identify genre and purpose; give insightful interpretation; explain relationships	Literary sample	identify analyze explain
AYA: Science: Exercise 3 Evaluate and describe a student's conceptual understanding of a concept and plan instruction to move understanding forward	Evaluate student understanding; describe two concepts; describe instruction	Student work sample	evaluate describe demonstrate

Create your own nutshell for each of YOUR Component 1 exercises.

Once you know HOW to deconstruct the exercises so you'll know what you'll be asked to do, you can begin to look for resources to refresh your memory of topics you don't teach.

WHAT WORKS! Using Component 1/Testing Center Internet Resources

- www.boardcertifiedteachers.org has many resources including certificate standards, scoring rubrics, the *Component 1 At-A-Glance* Document, and practice prompts. All of these provide important information to help you prepare.

- www.ecgen.org is useful to ECGens, MCGens and Literacy candidates. There are forums for each Component and for Component 1 exercises. This site also hosts weekly live chats and has an extensive library and archives. Information here is reliable and informative. There is a fee to access this site, but it is worth the cost.
- Yahoo Groups: Some certificate areas have chat boards/sites that cover all aspects of the certification process. www.groups.yahoo.com/name of group (see earlier reference).
- Another excellent website is www.proteacher.net. This site services candidates from all certificate areas.
- GOOGLE! Go to your favorite search engine and type in key words that reflect the title of an exercise. For example: ECGen look for play; PE look for exercise science; SS/History look for important American historical documents; EMC/Literacy: reading miscues. Read information, make lists, search for strategies, and so on.

WHAT WORKS! Books and Other Resources

- Your State Standards. Research topics for grade levels above and below the one you teach. Read the Standards for the age/grade range of your certificate area. Make lists of topics. For example, for the MCGen Exercise 3, *Making Connections in Science, I found topics in my State Standards such as Life Cycles, Energy, Earth and Space, Motion and Forces, Climate & Weather, Properties of Matter, the Solar System, and Body Systems*. An AYA/Social Studies–History candidate might investigate topics such as *Government, Economics, Early Civilizations, Regions and Places, Human Systems, Population Migration and Exploration*.
- Book series such as *What Every Fourth Grader Should Know* focus on specific grade levels and include subjects such as reading, writing, or math. These are particularly helpful for Generalists and Literacy candidates.
- Book series such as *Everything You Need to Know about Science Homework* covers the major topics within a discipline. Although aimed at fourth through sixth grade, middle school teachers and possibly even high school teachers will find them helpful too. This series covers subjects such as American History, World History, Geography and Math, among others.
- Advanced Placement/PRAXIS/College Board Exam Study Guides

WHY THESE WORK! Using a variety of resources will broaden your understanding of the Component 1 items' intent and content—all the better to prepare you to do your best.

HOW TO WRITE FOR COMPONENT 1

The writing styles you used for the Component's Written Commentaries provide the foundation you need to address the prompts in the Constructed Response Exercises. You still want focused, to-the-point sentences. You still want evidence (examples) and rationales. However, because there are no space constraints—the only limitation is time—you can choose the format—paragraph or even bullets. Choose a format that supports your thinking and organizational style.

WHAT WORKS! Component 1 Writing Strategies for Success

- Start with the main points, then go back and fill in details.
- If you get stumped, restart by restating the question as the beginning of your response. This will jog your memory.
- Using bullets is ok if you like that style because there are no page limits.
- Match your responses to the prompts. If a prompt asks for two goals, put two goals into the response—no more, no less. There are no bonus points for adding more.
- Emphasize Standards, student achievement, and real-world application where appropriate.
- Skip writing introductions and conclusions even if you choose to write in paragraph form. They take up valuable time but contain no evidence.
- Use facts and statistical details you know to be true and back up with evidence.
- Cite examples. Illustrated evidence is strong evidence.
- Formulate and utilize cause and effect information where appropriate. This exemplifies higher level reasoning skills.
- Be firm in your opinions. Don't say "I think. . . ." or "It may be possible. . . ." Such phrases weaken the discussion.
- Include rationales. Rationales are powerful analysis.
- Respond to every part of a prompt. Omitting information earns no points.

WHY THESE WORK! Knowing what to expect, how to study and prepare, and how to write responses will lower your anxiety and boost your confidence. You'll do better if you feel ready.

WHAT WORKS! More Strategies for Success with Component 1

- Study! Refresh your knowledge with current information in your content area. Brush up on your weak areas and solidify your strengths.

- Keep in mind lessons you've done that worked well and use them as a basis for your brainstorming. You don't have to completely reinvent the wheel.
- If your test will include reading, explore different themes in literature used within the age range of your certificate area, and specific titles that illustrate those themes.
- Check your state's subject and grade-specific Standards to generate lists of topics.
- Research national standards for your subject area.
- Use your colleagues as resources to discuss strategies. For example, EC-Gens and MCGens, and Literacy candidates might talk with teammates about elements of reading such as miscues analysis. Pick the brain of the Reading Specialist/Resource Teacher at your school. Even HS/MS Language Arts candidates can benefit from reviewing these skills.
- Have some ideas in mind for differentiating lessons that show how you can plan for different abilities and styles of learning.
- High school and middle school teachers may benefit from studying Advanced Placement/PRAXIS study guides.
- Know the steps of AAT and be able to apply them to the lesson you "plan."
- Read the *whole* exercise. There are often several parts to it, each requiring a response.
- Analyze the exercise directions. Pay attention to these elements:

    - *Content Area*: reading, math, science, social studies, and so on.
    - *Prompt Materials*: a scenario, a stimulus piece, a document
    - *Action Words*: Identify, cite, describe, provide a rationale
    - *The Task*: Show knowledge of . . . , analyze student errors, give examples of. . . .

- Make up your own prompts for additional practice. Try designing exercises for different age groups within your certificate area.
- Practice with another candidate. Brainstorm prompts and create lessons to address them. Pretend you're testing and start writing with a timer set for thirty minutes. Then analyze each other's responses. Do this multiple times—you'll get faster and better.
- Budget your time. Think: thirty minutes for three prompts = ten minutes for each prompt.
- Have confidence in your own experience and knowledge. Use these to address possible misconceptions.
- Answer each exercise/prompt completely before moving on. Address all of the parts. Once you leave an exercise, you cannot return to it. Unanswered prompts earn no points!

- Use the Level 4 Rubric for each exercise. Study the rubric and be sure you understand each and every word in it. Construct your responses to satisfy the Level 4 Rubric.

WHAT WORKS! Even More Tips for Component 1 Success

- Take the exercises in the spring/early summer when you feel you are ready. Many candidates share that if they give themselves some time off after submitting the Components, they have a block of time to prepare and feel less frazzled and more confident. In the 3.0 version, Component 1 can also be taken at any point in your National Board journey.
- Choose and confirm a date as early as you can after paying your fees. This will give you the greatest choice of dates and locations and will help with your long-range planning.
- Read all Testing Center instructions carefully so you will know exactly what to take: ID, authorizations, supplies, and so forth, and what you *can't* take. The Center has very strict requirements.
- Dress in layers in case the room is hot or cold and do take the breaks offered.
- Take a test drive to the Testing Center ahead of your testing day. It will give you peace of mind to know where you are going and how long it will take to get there.
- Plan to arrive at least thirty minutes before your scheduled appointment.
- Take the Pearson tutorial offered before starting the testing. It will familiarize you with the format and layout of the screen. Especially practice scrolling as each exercise contains several prompts and you may need to scroll down to see all of the parts.

WHY THESE WORK! With purposeful planning, you can approach the Testing Center and Component 1 items with confidence. Use what you already know about accomplished teaching practices to show what you know about your subject-specific content.

Chapter Five

Component 2: Differentiation in Instruction

Showing Accomplished Teaching through Student Work

Six-Word Memoir: Work samples reveal my teaching's impact. —Doug, CA

OVERVIEW: THE DIFFERENTIATION/STUDENT WORK COMPONENT 2

In all certificates, Component 2 centers on differentiation as shown through the analysis of student work samples. In this Component, you collect student work samples from a series of lessons, then describe, analyze, and reflect on the work of one or more students using work samples that show growth over time. The work samples, in the form of student pencil/paper examples, are the evidence of the effectiveness of your planning and teaching, your understanding of AAT and your ability to describe, analyze, and reflect on your teaching practice.

School districts currently require teachers to document student achievement primarily using standardized test scores. The National Board cares about student achievement, but recognizes a variety of ways achievement can be demonstrated. In Component 2, your analysis of student work is important not only because of the scores it produces for your students, but also because it is the way assessors will use to evaluate your teaching practice. When grading, teachers look for evidence in student work that shows understanding of the content. But the assessors go deeper. They look at your *analysis and reflection* of student work to see what *evidence of effective teaching* it provides.

The measure of accomplished teaching is its capacity to impact student learning. Effective teaching means, that as a result of your teaching practice, student achievement improves. This is why you'll plan engaging, appropriate lessons for *these students, at this time, in this setting*. This is why you'll choose the student and work you'll feature very carefully. The focus of Component 2 is on your teaching, not on student achievement, but if you choose to feature a student who did not show improvement—or as much as improvement as you'd hoped—be prepared to explain why and what your next steps will be.

What Do You Need to Do?

Each certificate area has specific requirements, but all certificate areas will ask you to:

- Highlight your ability to evaluate learning strengths and needs for individual students.
- Plan and implement appropriate differentiated instruction for those students.
- Analyze and modify instructional strategies and materials based on ongoing assessment.
- Choose one or more students and/or activities to feature as examples of how you differentiate instruction for your students.
- Choose students with different needs in either their ability or learning style. This will allow you to show how you differentiate your instruction to meet their needs.
- Select work samples that demonstrate your approach to teaching.

Read your certificate's Component 2 directions carefully because in addition to the requirements listed here, each certificate has requirements specific to that certificate. For example, MCGens must submit samples of both narrative and expository writing. EA/ELA and AYA/ELA candidates must show their students as both readers and writers. Math and Science candidates must connect the activities they choose to a major mathematical/scientific idea. And because music is a performance subject, Music candidates show student work via video rather than pencil/paper assignments.

Understanding the Prompts

Understanding the language and intent of the prompts can be challenging. It can feel as if you are answering the same thing multiple times. The prompts are written to elicit evidence of the Standards in your teaching practice and to reference the steps of AAT—the helix graphic found in the General Directions.

Notice that the directions in the Written Commentary ask you to *address* the prompts, not *answer* them. This is more than just a nuance of language. *Address* means to write what is true for *you*, in *your* teaching context. *Answer* implies something more black and white, right or wrong. The prompts are designed to elicit open-ended responses that fit *your* teaching situation. They don't dictate any particular teaching style and most likely your responses won't sound like anyone else's because you are describing only *your* practice, not your colleague's down the hall.

WHAT WORKS!

- Take the prompts apart and analyze what they are asking for. Pay attention to the VERBS because they tell you what you must DO.
- Look for *key words*. Example: *Relevant* is used in multiple prompts in the Instructional Context. Look *relevant* up in a dictionary or thesaurus and refresh your memory of its many synonyms. This will help you make decisions about what to include in your response. Do this with other key words as well—even if you think you know the meaning. Sometimes a synonym "clicks" with our brain and enhances understanding.
- If prompts sound alike, analyze them further. There is always something that distinguishes one from another. Sometimes one *builds* upon a previous prompt and takes it deeper. Or, in some certificate areas, similar prompts elicit responses about a student in different areas of the curriculum such as in the AYA/ELA certificate that uses almost identical prompts to describe a student as a reader AND a writer. Example: The Student as a Reader: *What about the student as an individual provides insight into his/her work samples and your analysis of them?* The Student as a Writer: *What about the student as an individual provides insight into his/her work samples and your analysis of them?* The question is the same; the difference is in the context/perspective.
- Notice that the prompts are connected to various steps in AAT—the National Board version of an accomplished lesson plan. For example, setting goals for a new lesson sequence is connected to Step 2 and when you respond to a prompt asking about the resources used to teach a lesson, you are connecting to Step 3. Evaluations connect to Step 4, thinking what to do next after an assessment to Step 5 and setting new goals for these students at this time is Step 6, starting the cycle all over again. Step 1 is always knowing your students.
- Address all parts of a prompt. Many prompts have multiple parts. The main prompt will be written in italics, but after it may come additional parts with specifics you'll need to address. Example: A common Instruc-

tional Context prompt is: *What are the relevant characteristics of this class that influenced your instructional strategies for this theme or topic of concern: ethnic, cultural, and linguistic diversity; the range of abilities of the students; the personality of the class?* This prompt asks for information about five characteristics and you must address each one—succinctly of course—but don't leave any of them out.

Planning Backwards: Plan with the End in Mind

Teaching a lesson, then crossing your fingers hoping that the evidence the assessors expect to see is there, is not the smartest plan. Your goal is to satisfy the Level 4 Scoring Rubric and *planning backwards* is an effective strategy to use. By that I mean to design your lesson sequence to fit the requirements of the Component, rather than trying to make the Component fit your lessons. Like planning a trip, you must have the destination in mind in order to get there. Getting to the destination is super important. Plan lessons that embed the evidence assessors expect to see into the lesson. This is not cheating; it is smart planning!

WHAT WORKS!

- Start with the evidence assessors expect to see. The Level 4 Rubric at the end of your Component 2 Instructions lays out the expectations. Example: Every certificate area has a Rubric Bullet concerning goals. Here is the one from the AYA/Math certificate: *The teacher sets high, worthwhile, and appropriate learning goals for students based on detailed knowledge of students' interest, abilities, and needs and connects the instructional sequence to these goals*. And from the ECGen Certificate: *The teacher sets high, worthwhile, and appropriate goals and objectives for children's learning that are tightly connected to instruction*. This bullet lets you know that the goals, objectives, and activities must be tightly connected.

Here is a fabricated example of poorly designed lesson plan that would *not* meet the Level 4 Rubric bullet:

- A kindergarten teacher plans a unit about pumpkins. *The goal is that students will learn the life cycle of pumpkins and be able to draw the pumpkin growing in its various stages*. They will read Halloween books about pumpkins, and write stories with pumpkin illustrations. The teacher sets up centers where students can see inside a cut pumpkin, count the seeds inside, taste dishes made with pumpkins, and draw jack-o-lantern faces on paper pumpkins.

Q: WHY will this set of activities NOT provide clear, consistent, convincing evidence for that ECGen Rubric bullet?
A: NONE of the activities the teacher planned support her stated goal of learning the *stages* of a pumpkin's life cycle and NONE of the centers provide opportunity for students to show they have learned the *life cycle* of a pumpkin. The goals and the instruction the students received are not connected. They don't match.

- Highlight *clear, consistent, and convincing* in the rubric. These 3Cs should become your mantra. *Clear* means anyone can understand what you've written. *Consistent* means that important concepts and evidence are connected and might be discussed in more than one place and/or in more than one way. *Convincing* means that you've provided evidence (examples) to back up your statements.
- Read the bulleted list on your Level 4 rubric. These items are the evidence you need in the lessons to demonstrate in your teaching practice. Paraphrase and create your own list in your own words.
- Include evidence (examples) for each bullet in your lessons and show in the Written Commentary how they are connected to your teaching and the student work.

The way to show *clear, consistent, and convincing* evidence to the assessors is to use the student work samples to point out specific examples/features and explain exactly what you did and why. The assessors have only your Written Commentary and the student work you submit to use. These are the only things assessors have that informs them about your practice. The work samples do not receive a score; rather, they provide support for the Written Commentary. But they are the *evidence* that backs up what you write.

USE THE LEVEL 4 RUBRIC TO PLAN AND EVALUATE

What might it look like to incorporate the Level 4 Rubric evidence into the planning of your lessons? To illustrate a teacher's thinking process, using the Middle Childhood Generalist (MCGen) Rubric as an example, read the *hypothetical notes* a teacher might write when planning Component 2 to include the evidence from Bullet 1 in the Rubric. *The Level 4 performance provides clear, consistent, and convincing evidence that the teacher recognizes student's individual learning differences and past experiences to set high, worthwhile, and appropriate goals for student learning and connects instruction to those goals.*

- I'll pre-assess to determine where my students are in the writing process and then plan specific activities to address those needs.
- I'll plan differentiated writing experiences over a period of time that address the learning differences represented in my class.
- I'll plan narrative and expository prompts that my students will find interesting.
- I'll provide reference and vocabulary materials for my new English speakers.
- I'll provide choices to meet my students' various learning styles and knowledge levels.
- I'll post-assess to evaluate my students' learning and to inform my planning of the next steps.

You can see how much information about the teaching process is embedded into the notes—and how it references AAT and the Component 2, Level 4 Rubric. You want the Written Commentary to reveal the thinking that went into the planning of the lessons and the actions taken to put the ideas into practice. This is what provides strong evidence of the rubric.

First person is the strongest voice to use when explaining your teaching practice. It's uncomfortable for many teachers to talk about themselves. But in this case, it isn't bragging; it's necessary in order to explain what YOU do, what YOU think, and so on. A strong voice adds value to your writing.

Making Your Selections

Every certificate area has important selections to make. These include:

- The topic and lesson sequence to teach that addresses the requirements of Component 2.
- The activity(ies) students will do to produce the student work samples.
- The student(s) whose work you will feature.

WHAT WORKS! Choose the Students and Work Samples to Feature

- Choose students for whom there is something to say. Select students for whom your teaching has *clearly, consistently, and convincingly* made a difference. Choosing wisely gives you the opportunity to showcase your knowledge of students, content, and pedagogy.
- Select students through whom you can *clearly, consistently, and convincingly* show the range of your teaching abilities. This means that you have used multiple strategies to reach students with varying needs.

- Choose students who show different needs in ability and/or learning style. This gives you the opportunity to show how you can differentiate to meet those needs.
- Select students whose work allows you to *clearly, consistently, and convincingly* demonstrate the effectiveness of your teaching strategies through differentiation.
- Choose samples that demonstrate the effectiveness of your teaching strategies.
- Choose tasks/assignments worthy of your students' time and effort.
- Choose samples that align with and support the goals and objectives of the lessons.
- Choose samples that show students improving their performance over time.
- Choose complex assignments that challenge students' thinking and show their learning across disciplines—toss the worksheets.
- Choose assignments that feature open-ended questions or prompts. They are stronger choices because they provide more opportunity for creativity, critical thinking, and showing understanding. Most worksheets don't do that.
- Choose samples that allow students to demonstrate a range of understanding about the content.
- Choose samples that show progression through the topic and progress over time.
- Choose samples with meaningful feedback from you beyond *good job* or grammar and spelling corrections. The feedback should show specific guidance, if needed, which will help the student know how to improve next time. Example: *You used commas correctly in this writing!* Or, *Remember to use commas with words in a series.*

WHY THESE WORK! Choosing carefully allows you to showcase your strategies and the depth and breadth of your teaching practice.

WHAT WORKS! Save (Almost) Everything

Save more than you think you'll need. Save samples that are connected to the goals you set for the lesson sequence. Save:

- Evaluation rubrics—yours and student-made ones provide strong evidence of self-assessment and student engagement.
- Class sets of work or copies (color copies if the originals must go home). This will give you the widest selection. Date all work.

- A variety of types of work that pertain to your lesson sequence. For example, collect products such as research reports, opinion pieces, and journal writing.
- Save work from more than the required number of students. This will give you choice and might save you if someone you planned to use moves away.
- Take photos of work samples that are three-dimensional or too large to scan.
- Make sure work samples and instructional materials follow the directions for the type of work the Component requires and for all specifications.

WHY THESE WORK! Such examples showcase your thinking, strategies, and your exemplary teaching practice.

Analyzing Student Work

Planning and teaching the lessons that produce the student work samples show evidence of four of the Five Core Propositions and the Standards. They show:

- Evidence of your knowledge of your students. *(Proposition 1)*
- Evidence of knowledge of your content area. *(Proposition 2)*
- Evidence that you think systematically about your practice. *(Proposition 3)*
- Evidence that you manage and monitor your students' learning. *(Proposition 4)*

Analyzing student work is very different from typical day-to-day grading. Grading papers usually entails assigning a mark, score, or symbol such as smiley face or star, returning the paper, and going on to the next topic. But grading papers that way isn't really analysis. Think of analysis as *insight*—what you "*see in*" a student's work. Analyzing means looking at student work in order to understand and improve it.

- Notice *how* students show they understand the learning goal.
- Notice *which skills* the student already knows.
- Notice *misconceptions* about the learning goal.
- Notice *mistakes* the student makes.
- Notice *indicators* that the activity was successful or not successful.
- Decide *what the student needs next* to achieve the learning goal.

Looking for Evidence in Student Work

Evidence = Examples. When you look for evidence to write about, you are looking for examples in the student work samples. You are like a lawyer laying out her case. You say something about the work, then use the example from the sample as your evidence that what you say is true.

WHAT WORKS!

- Be specific when analyzing and writing about student work. *When Ian wrote ___, this showed me ___.*
- Add details to your writing to show your understanding of a student's learning—or lack of learning. This is how assessors evaluate your level of knowledge. For example, saying that a student *can't write* really doesn't say much at all. Instead, show that you know *why* the student struggles with writing. For example:

    - The student's thoughts are disorganized.
    - The student omits vowels when spelling.
    - The student omits punctuation and paragraphs.
    - The student doesn't construct a beginning, middle, and end.
    - The student doesn't give reasons for opinions.
    - The student doesn't include details.

After you analyze for specificity, plan your instruction to include what the student needs next (graphic organizers, spelling dictionary, lists, thesaurus, etc.). This demonstrates your knowledge of subject, how to teach it, your Standards, and evidence you've addressed AAT.

WHY THIS WORKS! The kind of analysis teachers do every day connects to strong evidence of what accomplished teachers should know and be able to do. You already know how to do this!

Composing the Written Commentary

Imagine that you've planned and taught lessons about an important topic for Component 2. You've collected stacks of student work samples that support the goals and objectives and represent the activities and assessments you planned. You've chosen the students for whom there is something to say, and their work samples and your notes are beside you at the computer. You are now ready to tackle the prompts. You are ready to start writing. But start where? Write what?

WHAT WORKS!

- Respond to each prompt with information that is true for the featured students.
- Discuss your analysis of the work and cite specific examples that led you to these conclusions.
- Break the prompts into parts paying particular attention to the *verbs* such as describe, cite, or explain, that will explain what *you do* or the *student does*.
- Pay attention to the *nouns* you are asked to address. These might include behaviors, evidence, or patterns.

WHY THESE WORK! Component 2 is really about examining how you differentiate your teaching practice through the lens of student work samples. Analyzing student work is among the most important things teachers do because it has such a significant impact on student learning and should have an impact on planning next steps. You are already experienced with this skill! But you may not have had to analyze and reflect on it in written form until now. Writing clearly, consistently, and convincingly showcases your accomplished teaching. This Component is an opportunity to let your expertise shine through.

Chapter Six

Writing for the National Board

Six-Word Memoir: Read, Write, Reflect, Revise, Repeat . . . Submit!
—Nanette, AZ

PRESENT YOUR CASE

Writing for the National Board is unlike any other kind of writing you've done. It's not like the creative writing you did in high school or college. It's not like writing the term papers or thesis you produced when you got your master's degree. In fact, some attributes of what is typically considered "good writing" don't apply here. So, what IS this type of writing like?

Above all else, writing for the National Board is *evidentiary*, meaning its purpose is to present evidence. Its sole purpose is to present evidence of your accomplished teaching. It isn't quite as easy as pie, but it isn't rocket science either. It's a kind of technical writing similar to what's found in text or non-fiction books.

You must make a case for your accomplished teaching in the same way a lawyer argues a case in the courtroom by presenting strong *evidence* (examples). You are the defendant acting as your own attorney, presenting evidence of what you do in your classroom. The writing you do about your planning, student work samples, and assessments are the evidence of your accomplished teaching. The assessors are the judge and jury.

THE THREE STYLES OF WRITING: DESCRIPTION, ANALYSIS, AND REFLECTION

Just as an attorney uses various questioning styles to elicit evidence, the National Board uses three types of writing styles: *description, analysis, and reflection*. The noun forms are the *results* of your actions. The VERB forms of these words: *describe, analyze, and reflect* tell you what you must DO.

Description Tells "What"

When you describe something, you tell *about* it, you tell *what* occurred. In court, a witness gives the facts in order to paint a clear picture of a situation. There should be no interpretation or judgment in descriptive writing. In the National Board Components, you respond with enough information for the assessor to form a picture or impression of what you want to depict. Key words in prompts that ask for description include:

- Tell, Explain, List, Describe, What

A descriptive passage:

- Tells or retells the main facts.
- Is logically ordered.
- Has enough detail to set the scene and give assessors a basic sense of the class, student, or situation you need to describe.
- Contains accurate, precise enumeration where appropriate.
- Includes elements and features that allow an assessor to "see what you see."
- May be used in conjunction with analysis. You often need to describe the subject or situation you are analyzing so that it is visible to the assessor, thus making the analysis more meaningful. But the borders between them can be fuzzy.

Description is the easiest type of writing to do. Most teachers find description easy to write and typically tend to describe way too much. Although it is important to use description to give the facts and paint a picture of your class, students, and activities, it isn't the most important type of writing. Why? *It is the least evidentiary of the writing styles*. Description sets the tone, draws a picture, and gives the facts. But it doesn't deliver much, if any, evidence. That is the task of analysis and reflection.

The Instructional Context

The Instructional Context (IC) of Component 2 is the largest predominately descriptive passage you will write. This section gives assessors a sense of your teaching context and the featured class and student(s). Tell enough to give the assessors a realistic picture of the characteristics that shape your teaching context and the personality of the class. Be sure to respond to every part of each question, but *keep to the page limits suggested* because you'll need space later for other, more evidence-rich sections. The IC is often the place where candidates "learn" to write in the National Board "style." In most certificates, the IC is one page (check YOUR certificate instructions), and it's harder than it looks to respond to all the prompts in that short space. Here is a hypothetical passage that might represent an early draft/response to a prompt in the IC:

- My class includes one student who is identified as gifted, four students who learn English as a Second Oral Language (ESOL), three students who have been are identified as high-risk and are a part of the Early Intervention Program (EIP), two students who receive Special Education services for Speech and Language, and three students who have an Individualized Education Plan (IEP) for ADHD, Autism, Asperger's Syndrome, Fetal Alcohol Syndrome (FAS), and Bi-Polar Disorder. My class goes to specials in the morning, so my schedule does not allow for an uninterrupted literacy block until in the afternoon. I plan my literacy activities during a time when I have ESOL support from the ESOL teacher. During this time my students with special needs have the support of a paraprofessional, Special Education teacher, and Occupational Therapist. This support is imperative in that the ESOL students require small group and/or one-on-one assistance in reading and the students with special needs require support from a paraprofessional to stay on task. The Special Education teacher and Occupational Therapist are present during the literacy block to ensure that the students who have an IEP receive appropriate accommodations. (14 lines)

This is written well enough and gives important information. However, it's too long for the space available. Here is that same passage edited:

- My class includes one gifted student, four English as a Second Oral Language (ESOL) students, three high-risk students who are part of the Early Intervention Program (EIP), two Speech and Language students, and three students with Individualized Education Plans (IEP) for ADHD, Autism, Asperger's Syndrome, Fetal Alcohol Syndrome, and Bi-Polar Disorder. I schedule an uninterrupted literacy block in the afternoon when the ESOL and Special Education teachers, a paraprofessional, and Occupational Therapist are present to provide small group and/or 1-1 help so special needs students can stay on task, and those with an IEP receive are accommodated. (7 lines)

The original was cut in half without losing the most pertinent information. Saving seven lines on a single prompt can go a long way toward keeping the

IC short and sweet. Just the facts, ma'am! This is not the place for long explanations. Notice that almost every sentence follows the subject/verb pattern. This is how to fit more information into fewer lines.

Following are two more hypothetical examples of the succinct style of writing to use whenever description is called for.

- The featured class consists of twenty-seven students, who are a mix of sophomores and juniors meets first period. Several students are habitually tardy, making it difficult to begin instruction on time. Seven students are English Language Learners who leave ten minutes early to go to the Resource Room for language instruction. Therefore I must complete the essential lesson elements before they go.
- Jenny is both young and immature for a fourth grader. She reads on a second-grade level and has trouble putting her thoughts on paper. She often misspells words and writes entire stories without using any punctuation. She likes to work with a partner but has difficulty staying focused on the task.

Now read this example and see how you might edit it for space:

- This is a World History class of thirty-one juniors and seniors. Only five students read above an eighth-grade level which presents challenges when reading texts, researching, writing, and doing projects. Eight students have IEPs for Attention Deficit Disorder and one is diagnosed with an Obsessive Compulsive Disorder. My classroom is located in a "portable" building away from the main building which makes it difficult to arrive on time and so contributes to tardiness. I've arranged desks in groups of three to five so everyone has a clear view of the Smartboard. I have a document camera, a Smartboard, and two computers in the classroom. I take the class to a computer lab when more computers are needed. Periods last fifty minutes and this class meets immediately after lunch which means that many students become sleepy after eating, making paying attention more difficult.

WHAT WORKS! Keep These Points in Mind When Describing

- Be succinct. Say enough to paint the picture then stop.
- Decide which facts and details are significant and emphasize those.
- Concentrate on facts and details that show an impact on teaching or learning.
- Resist the urge to tell *everything*. Details matter but don't go on and on.
- Description should be the smallest portion of your writing.

- Follow suggested page limits. They are there for a reason—to keep you from using too much space for description, then not having enough space for analysis and reflection.
- Support description with specific details and examples.
- Eliminate words such as *that* and *very.*
- Use numerals instead of words.
- You can eliminate paragraphs, but as a courtesy to the assessor, *bold the first few words* when you change prompts. This helps the assessor keep track of your responses to each prompt.

Analysis Asks "So What" and "Why?"

Description is the writing style that tells *"what."* Analysis is the writing style that asks *"so what?"* and *"why?"* Compare it to an attorney who puts forth a theory, then goes about confirming or rejecting it depending on the evidence. Teachers make hundreds of decisions each day that are implicit in their knowledge of their students and content area, but rarely need to express this knowledge orally or in writing. However, the analysis questions require this intrinsic knowledge be put into words on paper. Analytical writing is important because:

- It is the most evidentiary of the three styles.
- It demonstrates significance: *so what?*
- It shows the assessor the reasons and motives (rationale) for your actions and decisions.
- It interprets and justifies actions and decisions—backed up with evidence.
- It shows the assessor the thought processes you used to reach decisions.
- It examines why elements or events are described in certain ways.
- It involves taking apart what occurred during a teaching event.

Prompts that ask for analysis may contain these key words:

- How? Why? In what ways? Tell your rationale for ___. Explain why ___.

WHAT WORKS! Sentence Starters

- Because I know ___, I ___ (planned, provided, organized, taught . . .), which shows ___.
- In order to ___, I ___.
- I chose ___ because ___. There are several reasons why ___.
- This impacted student learning ___.
- The ___ on his paper showed me that he didn't understand ___, so I ___.
- Because ___, therefore ___.

- The rationale behind my decision to ___ was ___.
- This was significant because ___.
- Upon reflection ___.
- After observation ___.
- This comment tells me ___.
- It is important for me to realize ___.
- This is significant because ___.

More Sentence Starters:

- This activity prompted me to ___.
- I now see/understand ___.
- These comments indicate ___.
- This could be more effective if ___.
- I continue to reflect on ___.
- I focused on ___, because ___.
- To promote (extend, refine, etc.) thinking ___.
- I now have greater awareness ___.
- I realized that ___.
- The impact of this evidence was ___.
- The evidence of this was ___.
- The intent of my question(s) was ___.
- This helped me to focus/refocus on ___.

Clearly label your student work samples and refer to them in the text. Assessors will look at the student work samples and compare them to the evidence in your analysis. Typically, the assessors read your Component, look at the work samples you've submitted to see how they support your writing, and then read the Component again. The analysis helps the assessors see the significance of the evidence you submit.

Reflection Asks Now What?

The descriptive style of writing tells *what*—like a journalist. The analytical style asks *so what* and *why*, like a scientist. The reflective style goes a step further and asks *now what*? Reflection is like a follow-up visit to a doctor to monitor a course of treatment. Reflection is a kind of self-analysis that:

- Explains the thought processes used *after* teaching a lesson/unit.
- Tells how you would make decisions in the future.
- Is retrospective.
- Explains the significance of a decision.
- Tells the impact of a decision, activity, or action.

- Reviews instructional strategy choices.
- Sets new goals based on your analytical conclusions.
- Demonstrates your understanding of the standards.

Prompts that require reflection ask you to look back at your teaching practice or to look ahead and predict what you might do differently. Analysis and reflection often overlap. Reflective prompts may ask:

- What would you do differently if you were to teach the lesson again?
- What does the featured student's performance suggest about your teaching practice?
- Were these goals appropriate? Why?
- Did you design appropriate strategies, groupings, materials?
- What could you do next to increase student understanding?
- What did you learn from this experience that will help you do even better next time?
- What did you learn about your teaching practice in relation to student learning?

Reflection assumes that analysis has already taken place. A typical mistake candidates make is to retell, rather than reflect. When you reflect you *explain* and *interpret* what happened, then tell what should come next. You look backward, then forward.

Use These Pointers for Reflection

- Be honest. There is always something that can be done better. No lesson is perfect.
- Be realistic. Don't propose something that is clearly impossible.
- Focus on both strengths and weaknesses of a lesson. No lesson is a total failure.
- Use concrete evidence to support your statements.
- Align and connect your instructional goals, the assessment activity and your reflection on the lesson. There must be total consistency and agreement among them.
- Focus on the impact your teaching had on your students.

WHAT WORKS! Use These Sentence Starters for Reflective Responses:

- In the future I ___. A key success was___. An area for improvement is ___.
- My plan for the next lesson is ___. If I were to do this again ___.

- I learned ___ which will help me plan better next time by ___.
- Before this lesson my students . . . , but because of this experience ___.
- Because of this teaching experience I learned ___.

WHY THESE WORK! The boundaries between analysis and reflection are not clear cut. Analysis focuses on *so what*, reflection focuses on *now what?* Analysis is about the past; reflection is about using the past to determine future actions. Understanding reflection will make your writing stronger.

Making Thinking Visible: Yours and the Students'

What does that mean? Looking for evidence in student work samples you'll submit for Component 2 is something like looking for diamonds in a mine. In this scenario, the *mine* is the student work. The *diamonds* are the evidence/examples found within the work or video. Some mines are rich in diamonds, others not so much so. Sometimes the diamonds are buried deep and are hard to dig out. Other mines have abundant diamonds near the surface that make them easy to find. You want to offer the assessors a *mine* that has diamonds that are easy to find.

The first step is to design lesson sequences/assignments/activities that will SHOW the thinking your students are doing. Build in OPPORTUNITIES to make evidence of student thinking visible. In student work, construct a plan that produces an artifact that allows the student's thinking and reasoning to show. EXAMPLE: Students are studying a math topic. They do a worksheet for practice. Within the sheet, they choose three problems to describe in their math journal or on the bottom or back of the sheet. They show in words and/or pictures how they arrived at their answer. Just the worksheet alone might show if they understand the concept or not, but wouldn't give insight into how they've organized their thinking or to any misconceptions they might have. Adding the journal explanation gives the teacher insight into the student's thinking.

What Works!

- Making student thinking evident gives you evidence to write about.
- *Make your thinking evident too*: In the Written Commentary, the prompts allow you to explain YOUR thinking . . . WHY you make the choices you do, and so forth. THIS is evidence the assessors can "mine" easily.

Appendix

STUDENTS **(Step 1: Knowledge of Students)** **WHAT I KNOW ABOUT:** • **These students at this time, in this setting** • **Learning styles** • **Abilities** • **Needs** • **Prior knowledge** •	
SET GOALS **(Step 2: Set high, worthwhile goals)** • **Goals** • **Objectives** • **Activities** • **Unifying Concepts/Big Ideas**	
TEACH **(Step 3: Implement instruction)** • **Appropriate strategies** • **Activities support goals** • **Appropriate pacing**	
ASSESS **(Step 4: Evaluate learning in light of the goals)** • **Monitor progress purposefully** • **Assess throughout the lesson sequence** • **Observations** • **Informal** • **Formal** • **Remediate/Enrich**	
REFLECT **(Step 5: Reflect on student learning)** • **Effectiveness** • **Successes** • **Modifications**	
START AGAIN **(Step 6: Set new high, worthwhile goals)** • **For these students, at this time, in this setting.**	

Component 2: Analysis of Student Work

Prompt / Evidence from Student Work

Prompt / Evidence from Student work

Prompt / Evidence from Student Work

Prompt / Evidence from Student Work

About the Author

Bobbie Faulkner spent thirty-eight years teaching grades K–6, is a Middle Childhood Generalist who was certified in 1999, and renewed her National Board Certificate in 2008. She has been a Candidate Support Provider for National Board Candidates for more than a decade and has mentored hundreds of candidates in person and through online websites.